The Terrific Colouring Book for TEENS

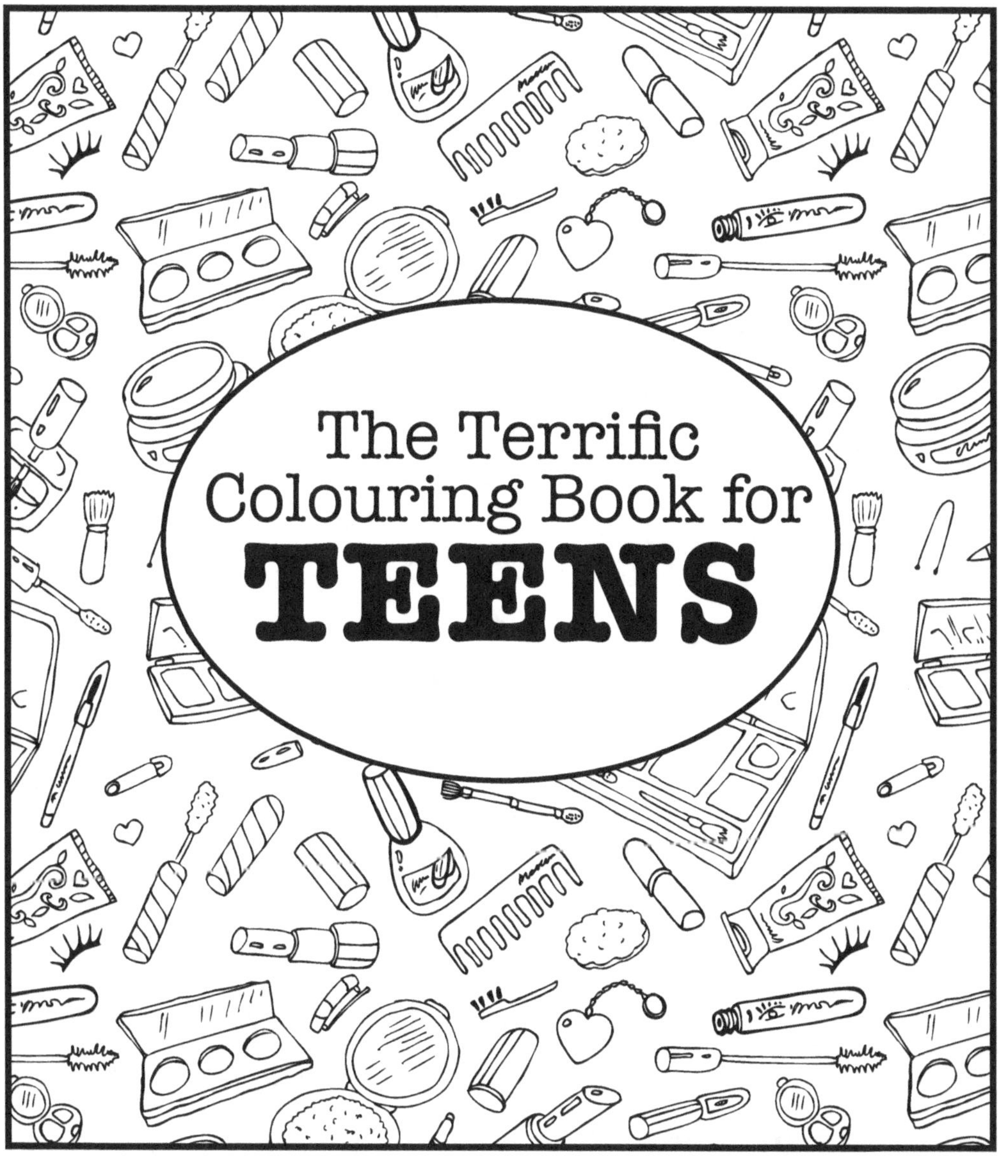

Really **Relaxing** Colouring Book

First published in 2015 by Kyle Craig Publishing

Text and illustration copyright © 2015 Kyle Craig Publishing

Editor: Alison McNicol

Cover Design: Julie Anson

ISBN: 978-1-908707-98-7

A CIP record for this book is available from the British Library.

A Kyle Craig Publication

www.kyle-craig.com

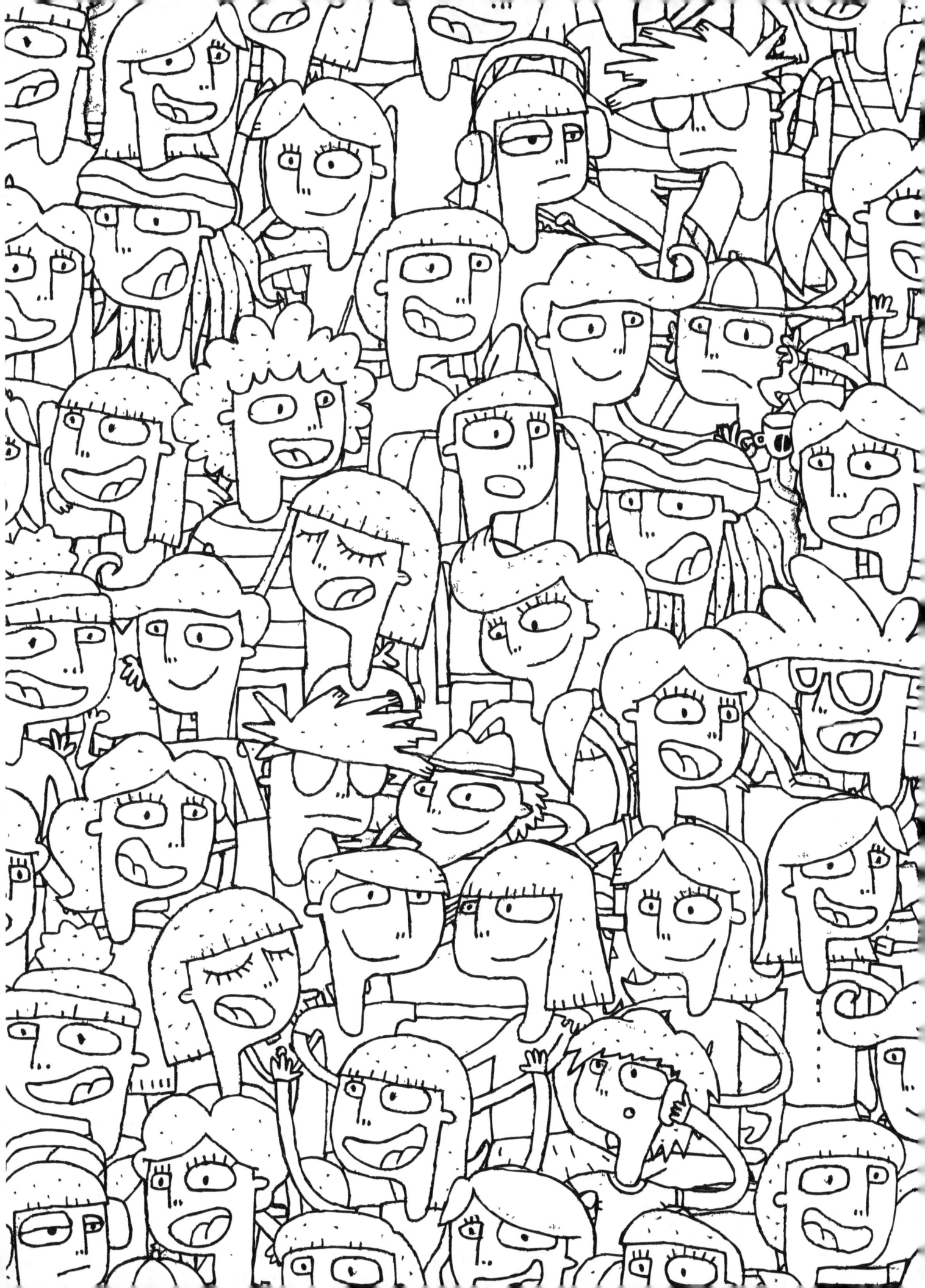

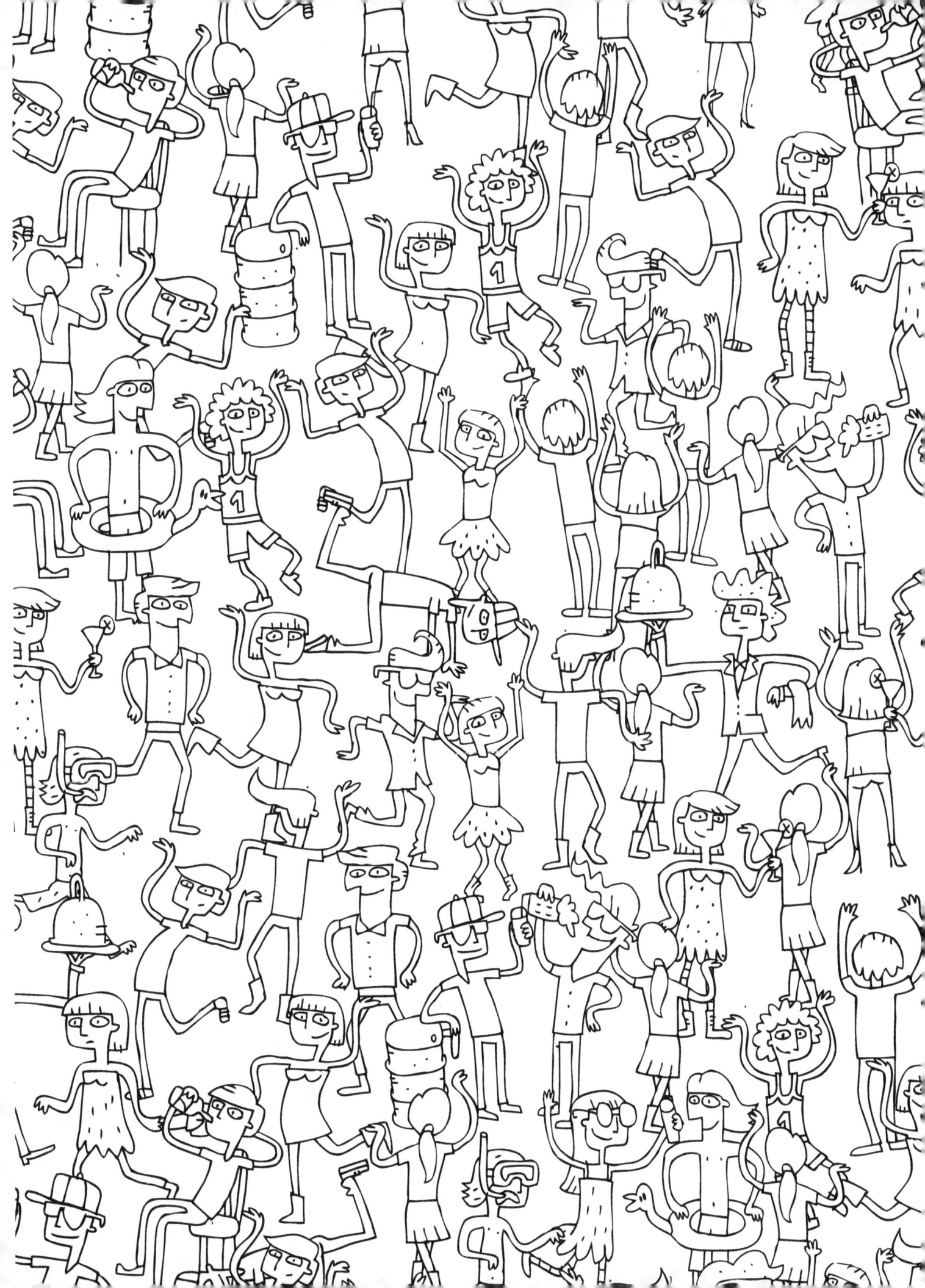

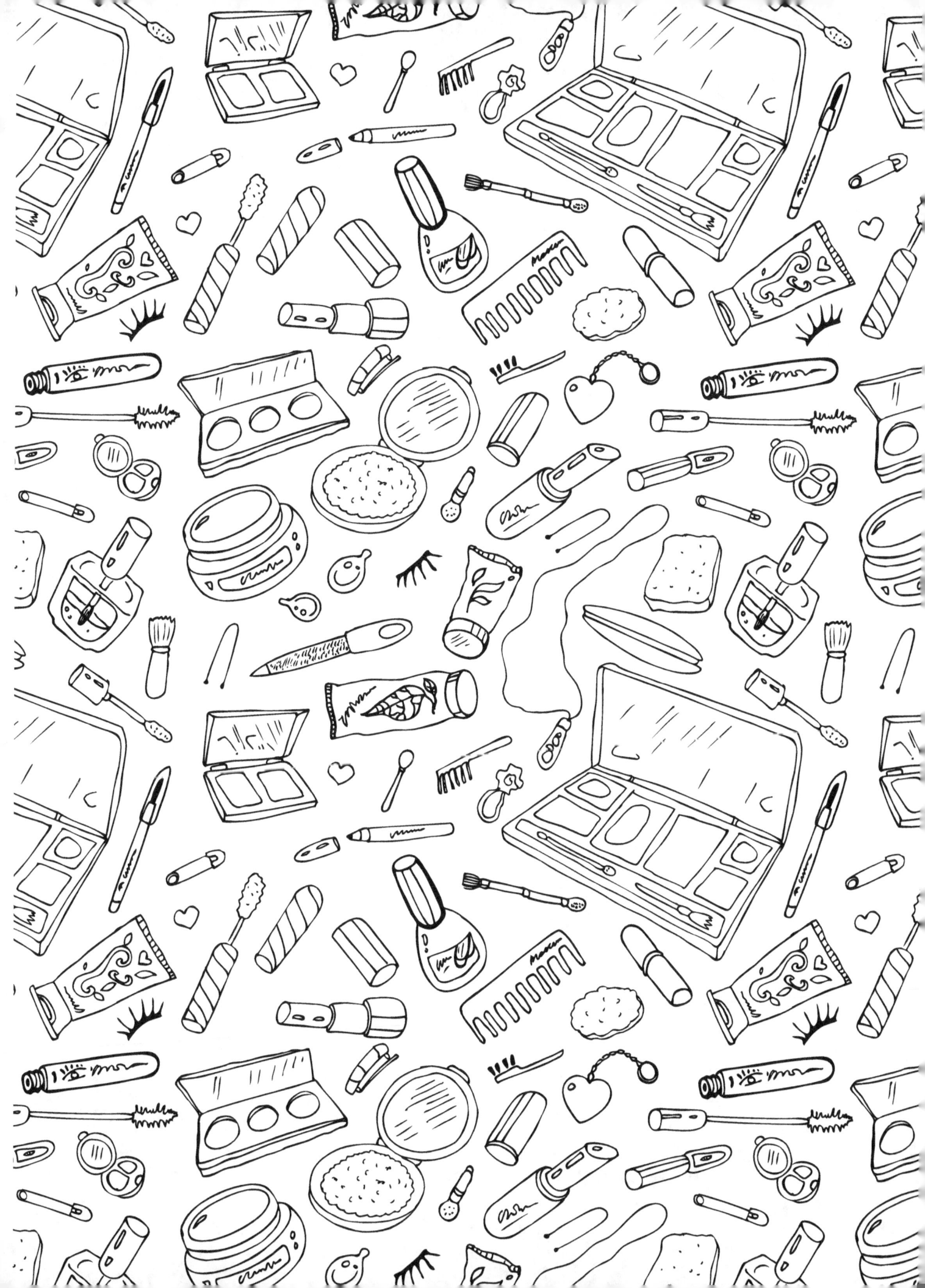

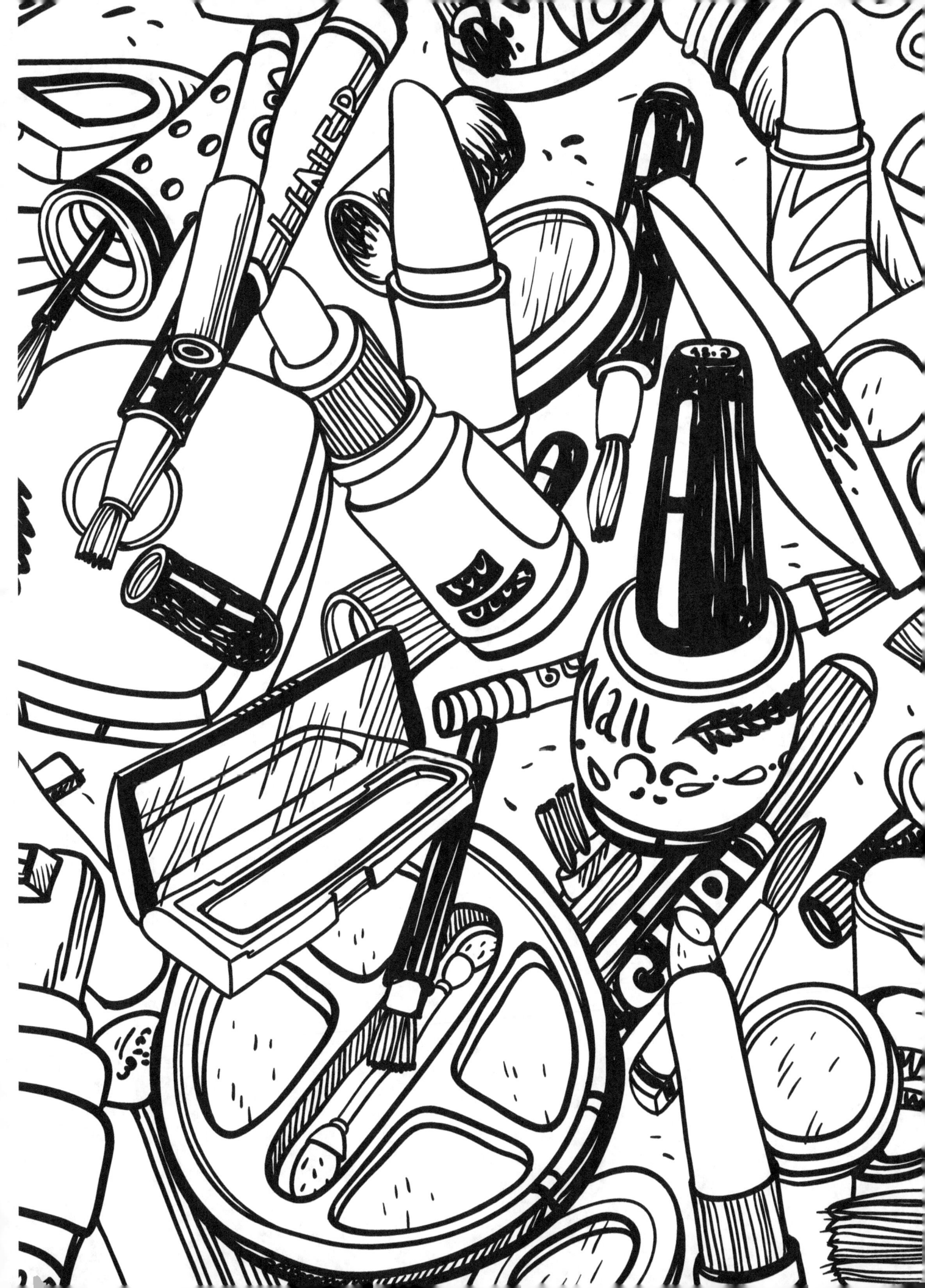